Published in the United States by Style Clarity Press.
www.styleclarity.com

The Style Clarity Workbook
ISBN-13: 978-0-615-61803-6
Library of Congress Control Number: 2012935867

Editor: Erin Foster Hartley
Illustrations: Quincy Sutton
Cover and Interior Design: Stasia Blanco

For bulk order prices or any other inquiries,
please contact marketing@styleclarity.com

The Style CLARITY Workbook

Table of Contents

A Note from the Author

Back when the television show What Not to Wear first started, I was an immediate fan. Who wouldn't want two frank and fashionable personalities to show up on your doorstep and give you and your wardrobe a complete makeover? But after a while I started to get a little annoyed with the format. Was it really necessary to toss out someone's entire wardrobe and start from scratch? How is this remotely applicable to real life? Even worse, I started to notice that every woman started to pretty much look alike by the final reveal. As the seasons dragged on, the goal of the show seemed less about personal style and more like some strange Stepford Wives experiment.

That frustration led me to start blogging and it didn't take me long to amass an awesome group of friends, made up of both readers and fellow bloggers. I was just one of many style bloggers who advocated for individual style and wore clothing from stores that most women could actually afford to shop in. But all things change, and eventually the majority of my peers looked like supermodels dressed straight out of Elle, Cosmo, and Marie Claire. Feeling the spark was gone, and seeing friend after friend close their own blogs, I made the unfortunate decision to take a break from the scene.

Before I closed down, readers often asked where I got my inspiration, or how did I decide to put certain things together. I would explain that I found the transition out of my 20s to be extremely difficult style-wise. Once I graduated from the juniors section of my favorite clothing stores, I realized that I really didn't have a cohesive style of my own. I turned to the style mags for help, but I found most of their advice to be way too generic and often completely unrealistic. I finally came to the conclusion that what I really longed for was an honest, personalized, and analytical process for finding my own personal style, so I sat down and came up with a set of activities that helped me do just that.

Encouraged by my friends' and colleagues' success with these same techniques, I decided to publish this workbook to help out any woman looking for her own inner style. I hope you enjoy it.

I would like to thank my mom and my sister, both women of great personal style, as well as all of my blog friends, past and present. All of you inspire me greatly, and I never could have written this book without you.

Thank you,
Bianca

Introduction

A while back, a fellow blogger (let's call her "Annie") sent me the following email:

> *I can barely manage to match my socks half the time—how can I even hope to own a unified wardrobe that expresses exactly who I am as a person? Is that even possible? I'm starting to think that the idea of any woman finding and maintaining one specific "style" is a myth perpetuated by fashion blogs and magazines to keep us all desperately eating up their crappy advice.*

Judging from similar conversations I've had with friends and female acquaintances my entire adult life, Annie's not alone in her frustration. We all grew up poring over silly magazine quizzes that tried to answer all our major life questions: Is my significant other a jerk? Is my sex life normal? Am I a good friend? Am I a Carrie or a Samantha?

Obviously, those of us no longer in junior high have realized that generic multiple choice questions are a ridiculous way to figure out anything about ourselves. But that doesn't mean that we don't still struggle with who we are and how to achieve the image we wish to convey to the outside world.

While I definitely feel for Annie, I don't agree with her assessment that finding one's personal style is an impossible task. My philosophy is that we have to find a better way to go about it. Just like finding the right career or maintaining a happy home life takes practice, patience, and a whole lot of hard work, so does finding your true style self. But once you achieve it, it pays out much more than you initially invested. In time, it may even become effortless—or at least appear to be, which we all know is almost as important!

Who is this book for?

- Women who are ready for some seriously proactive, non-judgmental tips for finding and embracing their true individual style.

- Women who feel like they have a basic sense of who they are fashion-wise, but need some help clarifying a few trouble areas.

- Women who like many items in their closet, but need help kicking it up a notch by creating a more cohesive wardrobe.

- Women who know they like a certain look, but continue to buy the same uniform over and over without letting themselves explore new twists or tweak the details.

- Women whose wardrobes have multiple personalities— and it's not on purpose.

The goal of this book is to help start you along the path of style self-discovery. I am not going to tell you what you should like or try to push products on you. Every woman is unique, and you deserve your own journey—whatever that may be. I'm just here as your guide—a Virgil to your Dante, if you will—but hopefully with much less drama. Together, we will uncover the stylish person inside you waiting to come out.

Inside you'll find a number of activities designed to help you do the following:

- Explore and build a basic understanding of what you like and what works for your lifestyle.

- Construct a style template that you can then play around with and modify at will.

- Make thoughtful, informed purchases and ease the anxiety of shopping with a clear plan of action.

- Cultivate a well-edited closet full of timeless, inter-changeable, and functional pieces.

- Develop the insight and confidence to stand in front of your closet and see endless possibilities rather than settling for the same old uniform.

- Achieve style clarity and truly *own* your clothing.

....

Create your own visual style... let it be unique for yourself and yet identifiable for others.

~ Orson Welles

One man's style must not be the rule of another's.

~ Jane Austen

....

What is style?

The dictionary defines style as a certain way of doing something. In this book, we'll be using the term to describe the way we ex-press ourselves through outward appearance—particularly through clothing. As you work through the exercises within, I encourage you to be inspired by things that aren't necessarily clothing related. Just the other day, I saw a car that was an interesting shade of green, and I ran right home and looked online for a sweater in a similar hue. There are no limits or restrictions here; no right or wrong answers.

As you develop and define your closet, bear in mind that every sea-son features particular "trend items." Style books usually tell you to avoid these like the plague, as they tend to go out of fashion very quickly. However, this style book is slightly different. There may be some trends that work into your wardrobe in a way that makes them more timeless. That's great! If these items reflect your style as a whole rather than just being something you are buying to fit in, they will not stand out as trendy. The freedom to break the rules is one of the benefits of *owning* your own style.

What is style versus image?

When we discuss style and image, and how the two relate to each other, it's often easier to think about in terms of corporate branding and customer perception of that brand. Companies spend ridiculous amounts of time and money developing a style (or brand identity) in the form of logos, mascots, websites, taglines and catchphrases... you name it. This is all done with the hope that customers will come to recognize this brand and everything associated with it and associate it all positively with the company itself.

So, what is image? This is the way a customer perceives that company thanks to its branding. Think of the television ads for Geico insurance—the cave men, the geckos, the weird little talking hamsters. From their advertising, a customer may assume that this is a company that doesn't take itself so seriously. Maybe their agents are laid back and approachable, and they'll help get you out of a jam with a smile and a little joke to lighten the mood. That's the image the company wants you to have of them. Whether or not it's really true—who knows?

Now consider the Allstate ads featuring spokesperson Dennis Haysbert. He's the actor with the friendly face and a deep, soothing voice. Personally, I'm drawn to these ads because they unconsciously make me feel safe and secure, which I expect from an insurance company. But other people may be more persuaded by Geico's happy-go-lucky style. Which company has the best insurance? Based on these ads, it's impossible to tell. But we've found ourselves discussing them based on their image because humans are drawn to that sort of thing. Like it or not—we just can't help it.

As individuals, our style is the outward expression of the clothes and accessories we choose to wear, and hopefully this personal style supports our image—the feelings and opinions we want people to have about us based on our appearance.

What does having Style Clarity mean?

Having style clarity means that you have a defined, carefully crafted vision for what you want to look like—and what image you convey to others. And on a practical level, you will know which clothing items fit your image and look, and which ones don't, saving you time, money, and sanity.

Sound good? Then let's get started!

SECTION ONE:
Get Inspired

READ: Where to find style inspiration

ACTIVITY 1: Find inspiration in everyday things

REAL WOMEN SPEAK: What inspires you?

ACTIVITY 2: Find inspiration in the fashion world

ACTIVITY 3: Find inspiration in style icons

REAL WOMEN SPEAK: Who inspires you?

ACTIVITY 4: Identify your current style

GET CRITICAL: How does your style inspiration compare to your actual style?

One of my favorite possessions is this Wonder Woman coffee mug. It's nothing really special—just a little $10 piece of junk I found in a local shop—but the moment I saw it, I knew it had to be mine. She looks so confident—so ready to kick major butt at any moment. It made me realize that's how I want to look and feel every day. So now the mug sits on my desk, holding my pens and reminding me how important confidence is to my personal style.

Where to find style inspiration

Now that you've decided to embark on the journey to style clarity, the first step is to simply start observing your everyday surroundings for potential inspiration. This section will help you develop the necessary skills to find style inspiration in anything, anywhere. There are lots of little bits of style all around, but unless we are looking for them, they are easy to miss. It may be in anything: from an ad on the Metro, to a shirt in a store window, to a CD cover. A little later in the chapter, I'll provide a list of everyday things and places that I find inspiring. Feel free to follow my suggestions or turn in your own direction.

Whenever an interesting object catches your eye, try to consciously identify what about it interests you. Are you genuinely attracted to its aesthetic, maybe even recognizing a bit of your own personality in it, or is it simply just something that is odd or interesting to look at? This is an important distinction to make, and it will save you a lot of headaches in the long run. A good friend of mine has a funny story—she decided it would be a spectacular idea to get Kiefer Sutherland's spiky haircut from *The Lost Boys*. As it turns out, she confused being *attracted* to a movie character with wanting to be *like* him and had to suffer six months of being called "Spike" until her hair grew out.

If you find an item and it turns out that you really do connect to it on a personal style level, make a list of all the possible reasons it speaks to you. This may include its color, shape, line, symmetry, texture, the mood it evokes, or even the perceived social status of the item. Make a habit of doing this every time your eye is attracted to something new, even if it's just in your head as you're walking down the street. When repeated enough, these small activities will help sharpen your eye for detail, and you may even notice some patterns or similarities developing in your personal taste.

When you feel ready to begin analyzing your own style inspirations on a deeper level, go ahead and complete the following four exercises. Don't be afraid to work at your own pace for each one, whether it's a few minutes or a few weeks. There's also no right or wrong order in which to do the first three—you can start with the one that most intrigues you, or you can work on all of them concurrently. Just be sure to save the Get Critical portion for last.

Oh, and one final note: I know these activities work because I've done them myself. You can find my own completed personal worksheets in each section. I've included them just in case you're curious to see the journey I took to find my own style clarity. Feel free to disregard these or study them as you see fit. What's most important here is your experience!

ACTIVITY ONE:

Find Inspiration in Everyday Things

For this activity, you'll need to collect 5-7 everyday things (or images of those things) that speak to you through their design. These should not be clothing related (that will come later) since our goal at the moment is to think outside of fashion.

To start, think about some things you may have around the house that you bought solely based on design. This may be a notebook from Target, a small vase, a photo frame, or a table runner. If you've had your eye on a certain something for your home but haven't yet purchased it, you might choose to include it here.

I have a close friend who has had her eye on a particular item of jewelry—it's a beautiful chalcedony and gold ring that is way out of her normal price range. But she thinks about it all the time, and is saving for it, and views it daily online just to see if it's still available. I would suggest this item go on her list.

Next, begin to collect images of each of these items. If it's an item you own or found out in your world somewhere, take a quick snapshot of it. If you found it online, grab a screenshot of it. If it's a textile or a color, try to get a sample swatch or paint chip of the actual item.

If you don't find inspirational things around you, then it's time to head off for a field trip. I've listed some inspirational places to visit on the next page. Go with an open mind, you never know what you may find.

WORKSHEETS

There are a number of worksheets throughout this book. If you don't want to write in your book, you can photocopy them, or send an email to worksheets@styleclarity.com. We will send you a PDF document of just the worksheets.

LOVE IT? PIN IT!

PINTEREST is a great way to keep track of your online finds. It's a virtual pinboard you can use in addition to your real notebook for the activities in this book. It's free to use, and you can spend endless hours viewing the boards of other members for additional inspiration. The great thing is it keeps track of the source of every photo you pin, so you can return to where you found it later on.

Check it out at Pinterest.com

Places to visit for ideas

Antique stores

Art galleries

Art supply stores—
(I can spend hours just looking at the paper displays!)

Bookstores—
(Especially the photo books and magazines sections)

Cemeteries—(If you're into that sort of thing…)

Comic book stores—
(Check out the graphic novel section)

Craft/fabric/yarn stores—(Textile heaven)

Cultural centers

Estate sales

Furniture stores
(Especially the swanky ones with stuff in it I'm nowhere close to being able to afford)

Historic areas
of your city, town, or neighborhood

Jewelry stores
(Diamonds or cheap beads—your call)

Museums

Open air food markets—
(Fish stands in particular can be mesmerizing)

Parks and gardens

Public libraries—
(Don't forget about periodical archives and microfiche. Bring tissues though—
it can get dusty!)

Record stores—
(The kind with bins and bins of old LPs)

Thrift stores

Urban centers—
(The architecture, the graffiti, the people)

Miscellaneous stimull

Cars—(Vintage and otherwise)

Commercial product packaging

Handmade paper and stationery

Vintage machinery

Movies and movie posters—(Pick an era or genre and dig in. My favorite is *film noir.*)

Old photographs and postcards

Plants and flowers— (Seed catalogs are great for this)

Travel brochures

Once you've collected your images, complete the worksheet on the following page for each item. After you're done with them all, put everything in a binder and move onto the next activity. We'll be coming back to these things later on at the end of this section.

....

Style is not something applied.
It is something inherent, something that permeates.
It is of the nature of that in which it is found,
whether the poem, the manner of a god,
the bearing of a man. It is not a dress.

~ Wallace Stevens

....

WORKSHEET:

A Few of My Favorite Things

Attach photo
or sample of item
here.

Item name:

Where did I find this item?

How would I describe this item if I was going to sell it? Write down all the words that come to mind.

What about this item appeals most to me, and why?

Are there aspects of this item that I can incorporate into my own style or wardrobe?

WORKSHEET:

A Few of Bianca's Favorite Things

Item name:

Cool house

Where did I find this item?

Browsing the Internet for homes.

How would I describe this item if I was going to sell it? Write down all the words that come to mind.

The Art Deco design is simultaneously modern and classic, unique, clean lines, cool/neutral color palette, strong but not aggressive, soft edges, elegant, flattering lighting.

What about this item appeals most to me, and why?

The clean but unexpected lines. It's uncluttered, fresh, but not boring. I feel like I could live a very simple but elegant life in this home.

Are there aspects of this item that I can incorporate into my own style or wardrobe?

Yes—the clean lines and the bright/neutral color palette.

REAL WOMEN SPEAK:

What Inspires You?

Liz, 25

The Fiorl dl Como sculpture on the ceiling of the Bellagio Hotel in Las Vegas. It features two thousand hand-blown glass shapes of various colors, and from below with the light shining through it, it's simply stunning. I love color, and the random brightness reminds me a little of a Monet painting as well. It just makes me so happy to see it, and I'd love to find a scarf or skirt that had similar coloring.

Tracy, 32

I adore vintage turn of the century photographs, especially ones that are mysterious or even a little creepy. It just gives me chills to know that this person is long dead, and this may be the only record of them ever existing. I can spend hours on the Internet looking at them, and whenever I run across any in antique stores, I scoop them up and keep them in a box in my closet. My favorite one is of this woman in the mid-1910s who seems to be a well-to-do socialite. She looks very bored and she's holding a monkey. I like to imagine she's since been reincarnated as Paris Hilton.

Carrie, 28

Right outside my front door is an adorable little pussy willow tree. Every spring I look forward to it blooming—the soft little nodules like kitten feet. My winter coat is extremely similar in texture and color, and it didn't really even occur to me until right now that's probably what drew me to it. I loathe winter, so I think I definitely need something inspirational to get me through those painfully cold months.

Marnie, 36

I inherited this old wicker hand fan from my grandmother, who I think got it from her mother. My family came from the Louisiana bayou, so whenever I see it, it brings to mind hot, lazy Sundays on one of those big plantation-style porches, drinking mint juleps and waiting for one of your gentleman callers to come by and woo you.

Chelsea, 34

This may sound strange, but I love wandering through this home remodeling store near my apartment. It's kind of a big warehouse with various kitchen and bathroom setups, and I love to imagine what sort of woman would live in each space, what she's wearing, and what things she would think are important to her life. My favorite of all is the huge free-standing bathtubs. I'm pretty sure I could handle whatever life had in store for me if I had one of those.

ACTIVITY TWO:

Find Inspiration in the Fashion World

Fashion anticipates, and elegance is a state of mind ... a mirror of the time in which we live, a translation of the future, and should never be static.

~ Oleg Cassini

For this activity, you get to start looking at actual clothing items that you might like to wear and own. In order to do this exercise, you are going to need some catalogs and magazines that you are comfortable tearing apart. If you don't keep magazines or catalogs around, ask people you know or visit the public library (but be a good library patron and photocopy or scan these images!)

Once you have a nice selection of magazines and catalogs, just start going through them and tearing out the outfits or items of clothing that you like. Make sure you check out both the editorial spreads and the advertisements.

If you don't want to use actual magazines (or if you need even more resources), feel free to use the Internet as your personal magazine. You can collect images from blogs, clothing companies, magazine websites and elsewhere. Try www.lookbook.nu for a wide range of style ideas. You'll want to print these out to complete the following worksheet.

Next, take your items and sort them into piles. Organize by clothing item, whole outfit, color, why you selected the item—whatever makes the most sense to you. At this point, you can get crafty and use your scissors and glue stick to cut out around the images you like and paste them onto clean sheets of paper, or you can include each page as a whole in your notebook.

This is an activity I recommend continuing long after reading this book and finishing the exercises, so you'll want to have a dedicated notebook or binder for this activity. You might think about choosing a magazine or two that you find the most compelling and subscribing to it. Or you can subscribe to fashion or shopping blogs that intrigue you and continue to collect style images that way.

Continually compiling items customized to your own taste will eventually build a look book that's all your own. Over time, you will want to cull the images to keep it fresh, but some will always remain important to you. I have kept an inspiration notebook for eight years, and I have a few pages from those early days still in the book that I still refer to from time to time.

ACTIVITY THREE:

Find Inspiration in Style Icons

Joan of Arc had style. Jesus had style.

~ Charles Bukowski

Style icons are a great place to find inspiration for your personal style because they not only already have a well-developed point of view, but they are also so photographed that there are lots of pictures of them for you to examine and collect. Sometimes with the true classics, you can even watch their style develop and evolve over time through their photographs.

Think of all the people whose personal style you admire and pick a few of your favorites. Now, keep in mind, you are not necessarily thinking of people who you want to dress exactly like. Rather, consider the icons whose style you have always appreciated for any number of reasons. And don't feel like you have to stick to celebrities—you may include family members, friends, and acquaintances, too.

I've compiled a little list below to get you started. It is not at all comprehensive, nor do you have to choose anyone from it, but this is a good place to start if no one comes to mind right away. Notice I have also included some men on the list. Style isn't just limited to women, and there's absolutely nothing wrong with incorporating masculine or non-traditional elements into your wardrobe!

Adele	Bette Davis	Catherine Zeta-Jones
Aishwarya Rai	Beyoncé	Celia Cruz
Amy Winehouse	Bianca Jagger	Cher
Andy Warhol	Mick Jagger	Chloe Sevigny
Angelina Jolie	Brigitte Bardot	Christina Aguilera
Audrey Hepburn	Carmen Miranda	Christina Hendricks
Ava Gardner	Cary Grant	Christina Ricci

Clara Bow	Jane Birkin	Oprah Winfrey
Coco Chanel	Jane Russell	Pam Grier
Courtney Love	Janice Dickenson	Peggy Guggenheim
Clark Gable	Janis Joplin	Peggy Lee
Crispin Glover	James Dean	Penelope Cruz
Cyndl Lauper	Jean Harlow	Prince
Daniel Day-Lewis	Jean Seberg	Princess Diana
David Bowie	Jean-Paul Belmondo	Queen Latifah
Debbie Harry	Jennifer Aniston	Reese Witherspoon
Diablo Cody	Jennifer Lopez	Rita Hayworth
Diana Keaton	Joan Crawford	Rita Moreno
Diana Ross	Joan Jett	Ruby Keeler
Dita Von Teese	Johnny Depp	Sarah Jessica Parker
Divine	Josephine Baker	Salma Hayek
Doris Day	Juliette Lewis	Scarlett Johansson
Dorothy Dandridge	Juno Temple	Serena Williams
Drew Barrymore	Kanye West	Shannyn Sossamon
Eddie Izzard	Kate Moss	Sienna Miller
Edie Sedgwick	Kate Winslet	Siouxsie Sioux
Edith Head	Katherine Hepburn	Sophia Coppola
Edith Piaf	Keira Knightly	Sophia Loren
Elizabeth Taylor	Kirsten Dunst	Theda Bara
Ellen DeGeneres	Kurt Cobain	Tilda Swinton
Ellen Page	Lady Gaga	Tim Burton
Fred Astaire	Lauren Bacall	Tim Curry
Frida Kahlo	Lena Horne	Truman Capote
George Clooney	Madonna	Twiggy
Ginger Rogers	Mae West	Ursula Andress
Grace Jones	Marion Cotillard	Veronica Lake
Grace Kelly	Marilyn Monroe	Victoria Beckham
Greta Garbo	Marlene Dietrich	Vivien Leigh
Gypsy Rose Lee	Mary J. Blige	Yoko Ono
Halle Berry	Michelle Obama	Zooey Deschanel
Helena Bonham Carter	Michelle Williams	
Isadora Duncan	Molly Ringwald	
Jackie Kennedy	Nancy Sinatra	
Jackie Joyner-Kersee	Nicole Kidman	

Once you've selected your style icons, your next step is to collect images of them.

Some great places to find photos of your style icons include:

The Library of Congress (http://www.loc.gov/pictures/)

Time and Life Magazines (http://www.life.com, http://www.timelifepictures.com)

For more recent style icons, try People Magazine (http://www.people.com) or InStyle Magazine (http://www.instyle.com).

You can also use Google Images, http://images.google.com or any other search engine. But wherever you find images online, be careful on what links you click on. Make sure all your antivirus software is up to date and activated to scan sites before you visit them. If any website looks sketchy, pass on it. You are sure to find the image elsewhere.

When you find a photo you like, save it to a folder on your computer or pin it to your Pinterest board. Once you have collected a good number, print them out on individual sheets of paper and complete the following worksheet for each one. When you're finished, put all the images and the worksheets in your binder with the materials from the first two activities.

Please note that most images you find on the web are owned and copyrighted by someone else, unless they are explicitly stated to be public domain (meaning not subject to copyright and free to use by the public). You may use them free of charge for your own private use, but you cannot republish them (either in print or online) without permission from the copyright owner.

WORKSHEET:

My Style Icons

Name of Style Icon:

> Attach
> your favorite photo
> of your style icon
> here.

What attracted me to this person? (i.e.
their clothing, their personality, or their attitude?)

Why did I choose this particular photograph?

What can I learn from this style icon to carry over into my own wardrobe? Are
there specific looks or items that are part of the individual's look that I want to
adopt?

WORKSHEET:

Bianca's Style Icons

Name of Style Icon:

Dorothy Dandridge

What attracted me to this person? (i.e. their clothing, their personality, or their attitude?)

Like my Wonder Woman mug, I think I'm attracted to Dorothy because of the confidence she exudes. She's strong and yet still feminine. Plus, she was a trailblazer in a world full of "no," and she demanded people pay attention to her.

Why did I choose this particular photograph?

In a lot of photographs of Dorothy, especially promotional or studio shots, she's smiling broadly at the camera, and it seems a little fake. I love the look she has here—it's both relaxed, as though she is getting a much needed break, but also very "don't mess with me." But again—still feminine.

What can I learn from this style icon to carry over into my own wardrobe? Are there specific looks or items that are part of the individual's look that I want to adopt?

Well, I'm not sure I could pull off a full skirt like this. But I like the simple elegance she embodies, and it definitely makes me want to really WEAR whatever is on my body and OWN IT!

REAL WOMEN SPEAK:

Who inspires you?

Tina, 31

Mae West. I love icons who were in charge of their lives and sexuality way before it was proper for women to think of such things. She wasn't happy with the roles offered to women on the stage and in movies, so she took it upon herself to write her own. She redefined plus-size sexy, and I think she's a million times more interesting than Marilyn Monroe or the other blonde bombshells that came after.

Jen, 36

This may sound a little strange, but I have to say Helena Bonham Carter's character in Fight Club, Marla Singer. I know she's a total screw-up and not a positive role model at all, but whenever she came on screen, I was smitten. Her hair is an insane, tangled mess and her clothes were probably fished out of a dumpster, but darn it, she WORKS it. Even with the competition of pretty, pretty Brad Pitt, it's no contest that Marla rocks. I want to be her, but without the smoking or questionable mental health issues.

Lucie, 24

Halle Berry, for two reasons. One: I'm super jealous that she's able to pull off the pixie cut. I would kill for her cheekbones. Second: When she cried and blubbered during her Oscar speech, I could totally relate because I become a complete mess in any emotionally charged situation (just ask anyone who attended my wedding, where I could barely get through my vows without a total breakdown). The only difference is I looked like a swollen, sunburned raccoon afterwards, and Halle still looked like a million bucks.

Michaela, 33

Lucy Liu, or any other woman who is not afraid to show off her freckles. I grew up totally covered in them, and I was constantly harassed by girls in my class all through high school. It wasn't until my early thirties that I realized they are a beautiful thing, and it's thanks to women like Ms. Liu (and Julianne Moore and Lindsay Lohan before she went and bleached them to death). It's like my trademark accessory that I never leave home without.

Jane, 41

My sister and I grew up obsessed with wanting to look like Debbie Harry from Blondie. We're from an Italian-Polish background, so needless to say we were never going to succeed no matter how much hair bleach we purchased. But we made due with torn shirts, red lipstick, and punk rock attitudes. Now my only hope is to age as gracefully as she has!

ACTIVITY FOUR:

Identify Your Current Style

....

The finest clothing made is a person's own skin, but of course,
society demands something more than this.

~ Mark Twain

....

Now that you've fully explored the inspiration you get from external sources, it's finally time to turn the lens on yourself. For this activity, you will examine your own current style.

For the next fourteen days, take a full-length photo of yourself after you get dressed for the day. Be sure to wear any accessories, such as your handbag, shoes and jewelry in the photo. If you come home and change before leaving for another activity, you may want to include these images too. Style doesn't end at 5pm!

At the end of those fourteen days, print out the photos and lay them all out as a group. Examine them closely and honestly, and then complete the following worksheet. When you're done with all that, put your photos and your worksheets in your binder.

WORKSHEET:

My Current Style

What items did you wear the most, and why did you repeat them? (i.e. they're comfortable, you just really like them, it's easier than picking new items, etc.)

Do you see any patterns developing in your clothing choices across the two weeks? (i.e. repeated colors, a similar style of skirt, common textures, etc.)

If you do notice certain patterns, how did you feel about them? Did you like consistency or would you prefer a more varied wardrobe?

WORKSHEET:

Bianca's
Current Style

What items did you wear the most, and why did you repeat them? (i.e. they're comfortable, you just really like them, it's easier than picking new items, etc.)

I wore my vintage maroon cords 8 times. I love them because they're comfortable, so I always wear them when I have a long day of writing ahead of me. I usually don't leave the house, or just hang out at a coffee shop, so I'm not too concerned about looking glamorous! I also tend to wear my black leather boots out at night a lot if I know I'm going to be riding the subway or doing a lot of walking. They go well with dressy clothes, but they're also a lot more comfortable than most of my dressy shoes.

Do you see any patterns developing in your clothing choices across the two weeks? (i.e. repeated colors, a similar style of skirt, common textures, etc.)

I'm definitely casual and comfortable, and much more colorful during the day, while at night I'm more professional or elegant. For my dressier clothes, I tend to prefer pencil skirts and black clothing.

If you do notice certain patterns, how did you feel about them? Did you like consistency or would you prefer a more varied wardrobe?

As a freelance blogger, I sort of appreciate that I don't have to be glamorous during the day when I work. Though I do sometimes wish my casual clothes were more sleek and refined.

Nighttime is a totally different story—I go to a lot of professional and social functions, so that's when I go all out and get to play dress-up. But I would like some more variety in those outfits, too. Black pencil skirts all the time get a little boring.

GET CRITICAL:

How does your style inspiration compare to your actual style?

Now that you've finished all of the exercises, take a serious look at all of the images and worksheets in your style binder. Consider the following questions:

Do you see a larger pattern emerging between your everyday inspirations, your fashion inspirations, and your style icon inspirations? Did you use similar words or phrases to describe what you like about them?

Do you see any major inconsistencies between any of your inspirations? (This isn't necessarily a bad thing, but it's important to note conflicting elements so that they can be harmonized later on.)

How would you describe your inspiration collection as a whole? Pick three words to describe it.

How would you describe your daily style based on your Activity Four photos and worksheet? Pick three words to describe it.

Now the hard part: How well do your inspiration words and your personal style words sync up? If there are huge contradictions between the two, take a moment to consider why. Are you too tired or busy to achieve your ideal style? Are you too scared? Does it seem too labor-intensive or expensive to build the wardrobe you really want to have? Try to examine these reasons honestly, and without judgment or frustration. You'll have plenty of time in later sections to come up with solutions to whatever issues you may have discovered here.

We went through several activities in this chapter. First, you looked for simple objects that inspired you and identified what you liked about them. Then you found clothing options that made you feel the same way. After that, you looked to other people for further inspiration. And finally, you turned the lens on yourself to see if what inspires you in life translates to your wardrobe.

Hopefully you generated a lot of ideas (and some questions) while having some fun in the process. In the following section, we'll begin to filter through some of this information and use it to reach your goal of Style Clarity.

SECTION TWO:
Get Focused

Breaking the style mold

In the last section, you hopefully found plenty of things to inspire you. In this section, you are going to take all of those beautiful objects, outfits, and icons and focus them into crafting your own personal style.

In other style books you may have read, this would be the point where you take a little quiz, count up the points, and *voila!* The guide then proclaims you to be a certain style.

Congratulations!

You are a TRUE classic.

This is the category I usually end up in when I take those quizzes. According to all accounts, this style relies on total perfection—a single wrinkle could ruin the whole image. How exhausting is that to live up to? (Not to mention the fact that it's completely impractical for anyone who's not a Barbie doll...) Oh, and never mind that the core color of my wardrobe is purple, even though "classics" prefer neutral colors. So what's the point?

If it's supposed to be all about finding your *personal* style, how can a generic quiz with five possible outcomes possibly mean anything?

(Hint: it can't.) So let's treat those categories as what they really are: a very basic building block for your individual style. Later on in this section, we will examine some of these categories in order to harvest some potential ideas of your own, but for now, I want you to think about how you actually dress right now, why you dress that way, and what it's really telling the world about the person inside.

ACTIVITY FIVE:

Find Balance in Your Ideal Image

My friend Jessica works as an assistant district attorney in a major city. During the day she looks lovely in conservative, neutral professional wear, but deep down she's really a rocker chick. By the end of the day, she can hardly wait to run home and throw on a pair of old leather pants and a torn band tee.

Every morning, my next door neighbor Caroline puts on a uniform consisting of cargo pants, a button-up shirt, and comfortable shoes before she heads out to teach preschool. But sometimes when I pass her in the hallway in the evenings, she is dressed like a glamorous 40s pinup model. I never ask where she is going, but it's definitely not to parent/teacher conferences.

Both of these women seem to have a pretty dramatic rift between what they like to wear and what they can actually get away with wearing in their "real" lives. The truth is, we all have rifts like this to some extent. We may be many things in our lives, either in succession or simultaneously throughout the day: wife, mother, employee, student, party girl... And our chosen wardrobe may not sync up with all of those roles.

However, I refuse to believe that this means that Jessica and Caroline are doomed to live double lives with double wardrobes. They (and we) just have to find a way to better balance those rifts within our overall personal style. To do this, we need to spend a little time calibrating our ideal image.

Remember from the introduction: image is totally separate from style. Image is the feelings and opinions we want people to have about us based on our appearance. In the courtroom, Jessica wants to be perceived as a serious professional, respected and in control. At night, she wants people to know she's a little reckless and knows how to have fun. In order to maintain a sense of both, maybe during the day, she'll wear a sexy black bra under her fitted button-up and blazer. And instead of wearing leather pants out to the club that night, she'll swap them out for a fitted pencil skirt. In both situations, she feels much more balance between her ideal image and her overall style.

Now it's your turn to examine your ideal image. Later on we'll work on ways to sync this up with your personal style. Consider the following list, and then move on to the following worksheet.

Aggressive	Eco-friendly	Interesting	Resourceful
Artistic	Efficient	Likable	Rich
Athletic	Elegant	Logical	Romantic
Comfortable	Feminine	Mature	Serious
Cool	Fun	Modern	Successful
Creative	Funny	Modest	Tasteful
Cultured	Good-natured	Organized	Traditional
Cute	Hard-working	Outdoorsy	Trendy
Demure	Imaginative	Practical	Trustworthy
Direct	Independent	Proper	Tough
Eccentric	Intelligent	Quirky	Unique

WORKSHEET:

My Ideal Image

Set a timer for two minutes and write down every word that comes to mind describing the ideal image you want to portray in any or all aspects of your life. Feel free to use the word list on the previous page, or come up with your own.

Now examine the list and narrow it down to the four that best apply to all of the many aspects of your life.

1.

2.

3.

4.

Lastly, complete the following sentence.

I want to project an image that says I am...

Great! Now put this in your style binder.

WORKSHEET:

Bianca's Ideal Image

Set a timer for two minutes and write down every word that comes to mind describing the ideal image you want to portray in any or all aspects of your life. Feel free to use the word list on the previous page, or come up with your own.

Confident, professional, smart, successful, thoughtful, open-minded, clever, fun, comfortable, classy, complex, tasteful, stylish, clean, happy, upbeat,

Now examine the list and narrow it down to the four that best apply to all of the many aspects of your life.

1. Confident

2. Comfortable

3. Intelligent

4. Stylish

Lastly, complete the following sentence.

I want to project an image that says I'm confident, intelligent, and stylish but also able to have fun.

ACTIVITY SIX:

Establish Your Style Boundaries

Now that you have a better idea of your ideal image, it's time to start working towards a cohesive style that conveys that image. The point here isn't to identify one outfit that is 100% applicable to every situation in your life. Rather, we're looking for ways to make small style connections between them all, like Jessica's sexy bra and pencil skirt. You can call these connections whatever you want—a structure, a template—the important thing is to establish the boundaries within which your style can come out to play.

If Caroline, the preschool teacher/pinup queen, were to do this activity, I imagine her discovering that she can carry over her love of 40s nostalgia into her daytime look by incorporating aspects of the traditional suburban housewife look—twinsets, A-line skirts, or belted dresses. She'd develop her overall style into a fun June Cleaver-meets-Betty Page sort of thing. Then, depending on the situation, she'd select an appropriate outfit which would fall somewhere along that spectrum.

For this activity, we are going to make a list. Well—two lists, really. The first will define all the things your personal style is or potentially can be (the yays), and the second will list all the things it is definitely not (the nays). Use your magazine inspiration sheets and your two weeks of outfit sheets for guidance here.

What to include (whether you love them or hate them):

Particular items of clothing (including accessories, shoes, etc.)

Colors, fabrics, patterns, textures

Decades or eras

Celebrity style icons

Fashion designers

Movies, musicals, or books

Cities, landmarks, architecture

WORKSHEET:

My Style Yays and Nays

My Style Is:

My Style Is Not:

WORKSHEET:

Bianca's Style Yays and Nays

My Style Is:

Pencil skirts

Turquoise and gemstones

Fitted blazers
and cardigans

Oversized
handbags

Ballet flats

Black

Solid colors

Modernized classics

Jason Wu

The 40s and 50s

Lena Horne

The Empire State
Building

Mildred
Pierce

My Style Is Not:

Harem pants

Diamonds

Anything
double-breasted

Little purses
with chain straps

Uggs

Neon

Polka Dots

Excessive styles

Roberto Cavalli

The 80s

Lady Gaga

The Bilbao Guggenheim
Museum

Rocky Horror Picture
Show

REAL WOMEN SPEAK:

What's Your Biggest Style Misstep?

Julia, 29

When I got my first personal assistant job, I thought I'd be so chic and wear heels to the office. I splurged and bought five pairs—one for every day of the week. The only problem (aside from the blisters and bruised toenails) was that I happen to have the coordination of a baby giraffe. The other assistants nick-named me "Clompy," and I didn't even make it to my first pay-check before I twisted my ankle and completely broke a shoe. Now it's nothing but ballet flats for this girl.

Renee, 38

I went far too long before I realized that low-rise jeans are just not flattering on my body. But for a couple of years there, it was the only style of jeans I could find. I suppose I could have shifted over to pants or skirts if I'd really been motivated to change, but instead I just gritted my teeth and went with the flow. I did a to-tal dance for joy once waists started rising again, and now I'm more aware of my body and what styles flatter it. Oh, and I've pretty much burned every photo of myself from the low-rise era.

Sage, 26

I pretty much went through my entire four years of college wear-ing pajamas or sweatpants. (I wasn't the only one, either. Looking back, it's truly shocking the number of girls who wore pajama bottoms everywhere, including class. We were a dumpy, frumpy crew, I imagine.) Granted, I was pre-med and didn't do much of anything besides study, but it still really annoys me that I wasted my prime hottie years swathed in baggy flannel and fleece.

Sue, 35

Until very recently, I would say the majority of my adult years were one big style misstep. I've bought into every horrible trend in the past fifteen years or so. Skinny jeans? Check. Blouses with those big annoying bell sleeves? Check. I even went through a baby doll dress/Uggs phase that I'm totally not proud of. Finally I decided that my clothes choices were telling the world loud and clear that I had absolutely no personality of my own. Now I stick to more timeless, classic stuff. I feel more like me, plus it saves me from having to trash my entire wardrobe every season!

Style Idea Starters

On the next few pages, you'll find descriptions of the more popular style types covered by fashion magazines and style guides. The purpose of these here, however, is not to simply choose one and declare it to be your style. As I said at the beginning of this section, you won't be finding any quizzes to pigeonhole you into one particular look in this book. Since we're all about personal style, it's a 100% personal process.

Like my friends Jessica and Caroline, most of us are probably a combination of two or more of these types. Feel free to pick and choose elements or aspects at will. I recommend you go through the style notes on each page and highlight words or items that resonate with you. This will prepare you for Activity Seven, in which you'll finally get to define your very own personal style.

Classic / Preppy

Classic/Preppy

DESCRIPTION: This style is distinctly American upper crust. It evokes the board room, the country club, and ladies who lunch. Work wear is very buttoned-up traditional, while weekend wear may be more casual but still refined.

KEYWORDS: Conservative, controlled, dignified, elegant, tasteful, timeless.

FABRICS: Cashmere, cotton twill, madras, seersucker, tweed, wool.

COLORS/PATTERNS: Pastels, argyle, cable-knit, houndstooth, plaid, solids.

KEY ITEMS: blazers, button-up shirts, cardigans, fitted sweaters, khakis, pencil skirts, sheath dresses, twinsets, well-tailored separates.

ACCESSORIES: Aviator sunglasses, briefcases, conservative pumps, glasses, loafers, riding boots, pearls, silk scarves, watches.

DESIGNERS: Burberry, J. Crew, Lacoste, Lilly Pulitzer, Ralph Lauren, Trovata

CELEBS: Jacqueline Kennedy Onassis, Katherine Hepburn, Michelle Obama

VARIATIONS: Outdoorsy, nerd/techie chic

Casual / Natural

Casual/Natural

DESCRIPTION: This style is all-American like the classic look, but it's much more relaxed—like classic on vacation. Hair and clothing can be fashionably messy.

KEYWORDS: Athletic, comfortable, on-the-go, informal, practical, unpretentious, youthful.

FABRICS: Cotton, corduroy, denim—basically anything comfortable and breathable.

COLORS/PATTERNS: Neutrals, black, solids, stripe—anything goes, as long as it's not stuffy.

KEY ITEMS: Breton tops, crewneck tees, jeans, loose sweaters, polo shirts, shirt dresses, trousers, light jackets.

ACCESSORIES: Ballet flats, book bags, coffee cups, sneakers, yoga mats.

DESIGNERS: Abercrombie and Fitch, American Eagle, Calvin Klein, the Gap.

CELEBS: Jennifer Garner, Lauren Conrad.

VARIATIONS: Sporty, yoga.

Chic / Minimalist

Chic/Minimalist

DESCRIPTION: The key to this style is less-is-more and totally understated. Clothes in this category feature clean lines and are perfectly tailored and proportioned.

KEYWORDS: Contemporary, elegant, expensive, luxurious, modern, sophisticated.

FABRICS: Cashmere, chiffon, garbadine wool, satin, silk.

COLORS/PATTERNS: Neutral colors and solids, solids, solids. The occasional stripe or polka dot may make a rare appearance.

KEY ITEMS: Blazers, button-down shirts, little black dresses, well-fitted trousers.

ACCESSORIES: Ballet flats, luxury bags, statement watches, stilettos.

DESIGNERS: Calvin Klein, Chanel, Donna Karan, Zac Posen.

CELEBS: Angelina Jolie, Catherine Deneuve, Tilda Swinton

VARIATIONS: Unisex.

Cali / Boho

Cali/Boho

DESCRIPTION: Here we find the sun-drenched Call girls and the wandering bohemians. These gypsy-inspired clothes bring to mind summer, freedom, and running through daisy fields.

KEYWORDS: Feminine, flowing, fun, laid-back, eco-friendly.

FABRICS: Cotton, corduroy, denim, hemp, suede.

COLORS/PATTERNS: Earth and jewel tones, batik, floral, ikat, paisley, tie-dye.

KEY ITEMS: Broomstick skirts, espadrilles, flowy dresses, wide-legged denim, peasant blouses, ponchos, sandals.

ACCESSORIES: Chunky/ethnic jewelry, headbands, slouchy bags, woven belts.

DESIGNERS: Chip and Pepper, Roberto Cavalli, Missoni.

CELEBS: Joan Baez, Mary-Kate and Ashley Olsen, Nicole Richie, Rachel Zoe.

VARIATIONS: Homeless chic, hippie, Rennaisance fair.

Rock N Roll/Edgy

Rock N Roll/Edgy

DESCRIPTION: Even if you're not in a punk band, that doesn't mean you can't still dress like it. The tone of this style is strongly anti-authority.

KEYWORDS: Aggressive, artistic, punk, hardcore, masculine, tough.

FABRICS: Lycra/spandex, ripped denim, lace, leather, metal studs.

COLORS/PATTERNS: Black, neon, red, animal prints, stripes.

KEY ITEMS: Band tees, hoodies, leggings, leather jackets, miniskirts, skinny jeans,

ACCESSORIES: Chains, Chuck Taylors, combat boots, fedoras, stilettos, wristbands.

DESIGNERS: Christian Audigier, Jean Paul Gaultier, Vivienne Westwood.

CELEBS: Agyness Deyn, Bianca Jagger, Debbie Harry, Juliette Lewis, Karen O.

VARIATIONS: Rockabilly, goth, skater, hip-hop.

Avant Garde/Artsy

DESCRIPTION: It may not be practical for everyday wear, but this style is fashion forward and cutting edge. If you can't afford right-off-the-runway couture, designers often scale down their outrageous designs as more affordable ready-to-wear versions.

KEYWORDS: Artistic, asymmetrical, daring, dramatic, independent, unique, unusual.

FABRICS: Crepe, fringe, satin, sequins, silk, velvet.

COLORS/PATTERNS: Anything goes!

KEY ITEMS: Blouses with asymmetrical necklines, high-waisted pants and pencil skirts, swing jackets, sheath dresses, unusual jackets.

ACCESSORIES: Cocktail rings, gloves, handbags, hats, unusual shoes.

DESIGNERS: Alexander McQueen, Dior, Dolce & Gabbana Marchesa, Versace.

CELEBS: Lady Gaga, Nickl Minaj, Nicole Kidman, Rihanna, Sarah Jessica Parker.

VARIATIONS: Mod

Whimsical / Quirky

Whimsical/Quirky

DESCRIPTION: This style is always the hardest to pin down. It often contains anything that doesn't fit in any other category, but the common thread here is CREATIVITY. Women who wear this style aren't afraid to toss together a little of this and a little of that and own it.

KEYWORDS: Creative, eccentric, fun, fanciful, individual, mismatched, playful.

FABRICS: Anything goes, particularly in multiple textures.

COLORS/PATTERNS: Yes please!

KEY ITEMS: One-of-a-kind vintage finds, skirts, anything that makes a statement.

ACCESSORIES: Bows, cameos, funky shoes, hats, legwarmers, oversized glasses, pearls, tights, twee handbags.

DESIGNERS: Anthropologie, Betsey Johnson, Marc Jacobs.

CELEBS: Bjork, Chloe Sevigny, Dita Von Teese, Helena Bonham Carter, Zooey Deschanel

VARIATIONS: Japanese street fashion, pin-up, vintage.

ACTIVITY SEVEN:

Craft Your Unique Style

We've done a number of activities so far that have hopefully helped you figure out what makes your style self tick. Now comes the fun part. You're going to take all of those lovely little ingredients we've picked along the way and combine them into your very own gourmet style recipe.

Take a minute now to review your style binder thoroughly for consistency. Take note of the things you want to keep, and cross out the things or ideas that sounded great at first but now you're not so sure of. Use these notes to complete the worksheet on the following page.

TIPS:

- Keywords: These words "define" your style.
  The adjectives describe the clothes, and the person who wears them. Stick with the adjectives you see repeated over and over, either exactly or in variations. Don't worry if some conflict or don't seem to mesh, especially if both honestly speak to who you are. We humans are complicated animals—that's what helps make us all unique.

- Celebs and Designers: List as many as you need to help define your boundaries. Again, they don't have to match!

- Fabrics/Patterns/Colors: Which ones do you see over and over again in your notes and collected images? What do you love to wear?

- Key Items: Your key items are the foundation pieces your wardrobe can be built around. These items will give your wardrobe stability and direction.

- Accessories: Include the standard favorites you can't live without, as well as some possible pieces you may have had your eye on but never got around to buying. Consider things that will adapt to a number of different outfits, but that still maintain your style.

- Description: Formulate two or three sentences that sum up the unique style you've developed above. Address the contradictions, quirks, or absolutes you've come to understand and embrace.

- Name: Give your style a unique name. Make it creative, fun, and memorable. Feel free to incorporate any of the popular style types from earlier, or come up with something entirely new!

WORKSHEET:

My Style

Keywords:

Celebs/Designers:

Fabrics/Patterns/Colors:

Key Items:

Accessories:

My Style Description:

My Style Name:

Now, you have a clear style guideline that you can use to develop your wardrobe. In the next section, we are going to put it into practice by planning/developing your wardrobe.

WORKSHEET:

Bianca's Style

Keywords:

Confident, Sexy, Well-put together, fun

Celebs/Designers:

Jason Wu, Stella McCartney, Aquascutum, Kim Kardashian, Angelina Jolie

Fabrics/Patterns/Colors:

Ponte Knit, Cotton, Wool, Animal Print (Accessories), Stripes, Lace, Sequins, Velvet,

Key Items:

Ponte Dresses, Cardigans, Fitted Blazers, Dark Wash Boot Cut Jeans, Geek Tees

Accessories:

Very High Heels, Bright Clutches, Riding Boots, Oversized Leather Bags, Silver Judith Ripka Jewelry, Leather Gloves, Scarves

My Style Description:

My silhouette is simple and body conscious with an outerwear piece (sweater/jacket) to finish it off—even in summer. I want to look like I might be heading to a party or get together at any given moment—including wearing fabrics reserved for special events causally with jeans. Lots of accessories pull it all together. It's not high fashion, but people admire the outfits I put together.

My Style Name:

Urban Tea Party

REAL WOMEN SPEAK:

What's Your Style?

Kendra, 34

I call my style Cool Rocker Mama. I've got three kids under the age of five, so the majority of the day I'm much more concerned with what everyone else in the house is wearing than whether or not I look stylish. However, when I do make it out to playtime in the park, the other moms find my endless parade of '90s indie band tees and my leather boots pretty fascinating.

Denise, 42

I'm California Hippie Chick all the way. I was born and raised in Berkeley, and I'm pretty sure my parents conceived me at Woodstock. I'm a midwife and postpartum doula, so loose clothing and natural fibers just fit right into my lifestyle. I'd probably jump out of my skin if I had to wear a blazer or fitted suit!

Belinda, 30

My friends have dubbed my look "Wall Street Butch." I'm a stock broker and a lesbian, and I just prefer to dress more like the rest of the guys in my firm. I was a little worried the first time I got up the nerve to wear a tie to work, but since then I've grown used to strange or outright hostile looks from people on the subway, and my peers have pretty much accepted me as one of their own.

Malia, 24

I'm Muslim, so I'm a little restricted with what I can wear and still stay true to my personal choice to remain modest full time. However, there's kind of a mini-boom going on right now in Islamic fashion. There are more and more interesting but modest clothes available on the market these days, and I love to dress in pinks and oranges.

Tanya, 27

I think you could classify me as Sporty-by-Day/Glam-by-Night. I teach yoga in the mornings and bartend at an upscale night-club in the evenings. I guess the running thread through my wardrobe overall is the color black. I can tell you this much—it sure makes it much easier to do the laundry!

SECTION THREE:
Define Your Style

MY BLACK PENCIL SKIRT

This skirt is probably the most beloved and versatile piece of clothing I own. It's comfortable and stylish, and it's great for both the office and a night out at a trendy club. Whenever I go shopping for tops, shoes, or accessories, I keep this skirt in the back of my mind (if I'm not actually wearing it at the time). If an item catches my eye and it is sure to complement the skirt, it's a keeper. If not, I move on. It's as simple as that.

Style is a simple way of saying complicated things.

~ Jean Cocteau

Style is knowing who you are, what you want to say,
and not giving a damn.

~ Gore Vidal

Establishing a wardrobe foundation

Now that you've defined your style and given it a name, it's time to start planning your actual wardrobe. Right now you may be feeling like your closet is just a mish-mash of random clothes you've purchased over the years, and the thought of organizing it all may be causing you a touch of anxiety. But never fear.

This section will help you develop a set of guidelines that will simplify the process of designing a wardrobe that is coordinated and versatile—one that expresses who you are so thoroughly that you will hardly have to think about getting dressed in the morning.

To do this, you'll first be establishing a wardrobe foundation. In the previous section, you already gave some thought to key pieces you already own or may want to purchase. These will become the support beams of your closet, around which all other pieces will need to coordinate. You shouldn't worry about these pieces limiting your wardrobe options. If at any time, you decide you don't like or need a particular foundation piece, you can simply swap it out for something else.

This section will help you define both your work wardrobe style (which is probably the most important area for many women) as well as your casual wardrobe. You may want to return to these activities anytime you have a major life event, such as:

- A career change or a promotion

- A relationship change (a break-up, marriage, divorce, etc.)

- A significant milestone in your family (childbirth, kids starting school, empty nest, etc.)

- Any other major lifestyle change (significant weight loss, a shift in diet, beginning a study of yoga or meditation, as a reward for dedicated exercise, etc.)

ACTIVITY EIGHT:

Define Key Pieces

For the following activity, you will consider the personal style you created in the previous section, and start building your wardrobe. You'll need to look over your worksheet for Activity Seven, particularly the Key Items section. If those items still appeal to you as foundation items, list them below. Or if you have identified other items since completing the activity, list those instead.

1.

2.

3.

4.

When you feel satisfied with your four central items, move on to the worksheet on the next page. For each of the items, answer the following questions. When you're done, put the sheets in your style binder.

WORKSHEET:

My Key Pieces

Item 1:

Why is this item important to your style?

What other items in your wardrobe will coordinate with this item?

What items have you seen online or in stores that would coordinate with this item?

Item 2:

Why is this item important to your style?

What other items in your wardrobe will coordinate with this item?

What items have you seen online or in stores that would coordinate with this item?

Item 3:

Why is this item important to your style?

What other items in your wardrobe will coordinate with this item?

What items have you seen online or in stores that would coordinate with this item?

Item 4:

Why is this item important to your style?

What other items in your wardrobe will coordinate with this item?

What items have you seen online or in stores that would coordinate with this item?

WORKSHEET:

Bianca's Key Pieces

Item 1: *Pencil Skirt*

Why is this item important to your style?

This item is important to my style because it fits well, projects an air of authority and confidence and is feminine.

What other items in your wardrobe will coordinate with this item?

This will coordinate with all my blouses, tops, sweaters etc. It will be a true staple.

What items have you seen online or in stores that would coordinate with this item?

?

Item 2: *Red Suede Pumps 3.5 Heels*

Why is this item important to your style?

This is important to my style because it projects the image I want to provide, and brings in some of the luxury aspects of my style, while still providing that pop of color I love.

What other items in your wardrobe will coordinate with this item?

This will coordinate with all my neutrals, most of my jewel tones and any pieces I own that are not tailored for flats.

What items have you seen online or in stores that would coordinate with this item?

Patterned Pencil Skirts, Denim, Brown Leather Jacket

Item 3: *Grey/Silver Sequin Tank*

Why is this item important to your style?

I feel the sequins show there is always a party in my wardrobe. The grey will tone it down so I can wear it casually. I want to have fun with the styling. I think by setting this as a base foundation it makes a statement about the rest of the pieces.

What other items in your wardrobe will coordinate with this item?

Velvet Blazers, Jeans, Pencil Skirts, Cardigans, All the jewel tones that I love.

What items have you seen online or in stores that would coordinate with this item?

Wrap style sweater, black walking shorts, flats with jewel embellishments

Item 4: *Fitted Blazer*

Why is this item important to your style?

Versatility of the garment + ability to dress up any casual outfit automatically makes this a must have for my closet.

What other items in your wardrobe will coordinate with this item?

Jeans, Ponte and Cotton Stretch Dresses, Pencil Skirts, Teeshirts

What items have you seen online or in stores that would coordinate with this item?

Sky is the limit.

What is your work situation?

It's important to consider the reality of your work situation before constructing your wardrobe. For some women, your personality and profession may dovetail together so perfectly that it's a no-brainer. If you fall into this category, then consider yourself lucky. For others of us, though, it may be a bit of a struggle to mesh the practical needs of the workplace with your creative personal style.

Below are some typical workplace situations. Consider which one yours falls into, and some of the ways you can begin to customize your style to it. Afterwards, check out the case studies to see how individual women have adapted their personal style into their workplace.

Corporate: This includes the fast-paced world of Wall Street, law firms, banks, and company boardrooms. These workplaces typically require the very peak of professional dress. As a result, you have a much narrower zone of style flexibility to work with, especially if your defined style tends more towards the casual or the quirky. I would suggest not rocking the boat too much, but rather exploring the realm of more subtle personal touches. Consider tailoring the cut of your skirts or jackets in an interesting way, or incorporating accessories that are stylish and unique without being too flashy.

Business Casual: This is a very broad term that is used by many companies to describe a dress code that is not quite corporate, but not totally casual. This category allows for a much more flexible integration of personal style, but again—you'll want to be careful not to cross the line of propriety. You'll probably fit in just fine with 3-piece outfits made up of separates rather than a matching corporate suit. Play with color, texture, and patterns, as well as shoes and accessories.

Casual: a casual dress code can be difficult for a stylish woman. You may find that any attempt to stand out or express yourself through your clothing will elicit lots of "side-eyeing" from co-workers—or comments like, "What's the occasion? Big interview?" Depending on how self-confident you are, these sorts of reactions may make you feel special, or they may have you running back to your standard invisible khakis and understated blouse. While there is something to be said for marching to the beat of your own drum, it may be equally important to you not to alienate yourself from coworkers over your wardrobe. In this case, I would advise a similar path as those who must toe the corporate line. Wear the appropriate casual uniform, but add bits of your personality through the cut of your jeans and the accessories you wear.

Work at Home: Once you get over the temptation to sit around in your bathrobe all day, you'll realize you're in the unique position of being able to totally embrace your personal style. Take advantage of that! There may be some exceptions to this, like in-home childcare workers or stay-at-home moms, but otherwise, the sky is the limit!

On the following pages, you'll find some case studies of women who work in each of these situations. They've been generous enough to share how they've found balance between their work dress codes and their personal style.

CASE STUDY 1: *Monica, Real Estate Agent*

After working for six years as a secretary in a Chicago real estate office, one day I finally decided, "Hey, I can do that!" I studied for my license nights and weekends while raising my two young children all on my own, and a year later—I got it! Throughout the process, I was lucky enough to have the full support of my bosses, and they immediately hired me on as a junior partner.

However, I wanted a way to let everyone in the office know that I was no longer just the woman who forwarded calls and made coffee. I took my career change as an opportunity to re-define my personal style.

As a secretary, I'd always worn simple mid-calf wool skirts and conservative sweater sets. I didn't particularly care for the look (I used to refer to it as the not-very-sexy librarian), but it was easy and affordable. But I knew this look would definitely NOT cut it as an agent. Our agency caters to upper-class clients looking for brownstones and condos in Naperville, so our office requires a corporate dress code that reflects upward mobility and class (no cheesy orange blazers, thank goodness!).

I faced an additional hurdle in that I was the first female agent the firm had ever hired. That meant I really didn't have a blueprint on which to model my new wardrobe. After doing some soul searching, I discovered that I was drawn to a style that bordered on classic/minimalist with a single splash of bright color. I named this style "A bloom in the desert." My wardrobe consists of neutral skirts, pants, and jackets, and I swap out various jewel-tone blouses. Or I may go all neutral and throw on a pair of lime green heels.

It took my boss and coworkers a few weeks to get used to my new look, but they've since embraced it. I've even noticed that the other agents are shaking up their Hugo Boss suits with a splashy tie or pocket square.

CASE STUDY 2: *Gretchen, Community College Professor*

I teach film classes at a community college in a pretty liberal Midwestern city, and while we don't technically have a dress code, pretty much all of the professors follow a pretty bland business casual trend. I'm one of the few arts instructors on campus (and the only film instructor), and over the years I've pushed the boundaries oh-so-slowly and realized I'm not really expected to be bound by the style status quo. But I have established my own dress code based on my personal style.

One item that is a definite must for me is a pair of heels that are no shorter than 3 inches. Something about them gives me a confidence boost. I feel like it's a signal that hey—I'm not just trying to fit in as a student with your average ballet flats or Pumas. On the off chance I do wear flat shoes to class, it just feels... *wrong*. I started teaching when I was 25 (looking no older than 19), and I often got confused in the hallway for a student. So I guess I developed a need to stand out as an authority figure.

Now that I'm older and more confident, I'm starting to get more daring in my clothing choices. My personal style falls soundly in the "quirky" category, but I also keep it professional enough that it's not too distracting to my students. I want them listening to what I'm saying, not sitting there wondering why my skirt is made out of Muppet fur. I absolutely love my job—the fact that I get to talk about a subject I'm so passionate about every day never fails to make my head swim. Over the years, I think I've gotten so comfortable in my skin that I've allowed myself to express the goofball side of me more and more.

My favorite outfit is a pair of perfectly tailored gray twill pants, a black sleeveless blouse interwoven with velvet and random black sequins, a pair of pink arm warmers (knitted by yours truly), and my trusty black suede Mary Jane heels. I feel like it says, "I'm professional and I know how to dress for my body type, but I'm not afraid to express my artistic side."

CASE STUDY 3: *Ruby, University Office Clerk*

I work in a Southern State University, the youngest worker in my office by at least fifteen years. We have a very casual dress code with a few exceptions (no sleeveless shirts or flip flops). It's an understatement to say the ladies in my office are out of touch with fashion. On any given day, it's a parade of unflattering mom jeans or Caprl pants, plain t-shirts three sizes too big, or sweatshirts emblazoned with our school's logo, i.e. totally NOT me.

For awhile, I let my freak flag fly with Mod dresses and other beloved vintage finds I've collected over the years. And very quickly, I just got tired of the titters, forced smiles, and condescending "Oh Ruby!"'s. But I refused to fall into their fashion vortex, so I decided to search for a compromise that allowed me to fit in while still maintaining my sanity.

I started by narrowing my vintage wardrobe down to more timeless pieces, and shopping for items that didn't immediately scream "Retro!" Over the course of a few months I realized I'd hit upon a perfect formula: conservative-casual 70s chic. A-line wool skirts, solid cowl-neck sweaters, and suede boots. Everything in muted browns, grays, and olive greens. And for some reason I can't quite fathom, it completely flies under my coworkers' radar. Maybe it's some sort of nostalgic fashion opiate that makes them comfortable because they already lived through it once? I've given up wondering. All I know is I am now happy in my relative office anonymity, and comfortable in my new personal style.

CASE STUDY 4: *Maria, Children's Book Author*

I grew up adoring Jacqueline Kennedy Onassis, especially during her years working as an editor. She was my idol in every aspect but her fashion sense, which I found, well... a little safe. Rather, my style icons growing up were Isadora Duncan and Greta Garbo. I loved Garbo's masculine sexiness, and I coveted Duncan's long, flowing scarves.

There are probably few workplaces I could get away with wearing English riding breeches and a red crepe scarf that hangs down to my knees, but lucky for me, I'm self-employed. Being a writer is an additional plus, as everyone expects me to be a little nutso anyway. Over the years I've developed a personal style that is both masculine and feminine, and without both I feel like my whole world is out of balance. That's probably one of the biggest motivating factors that keeps me writing in order to pay the bills. That way, the only one who can complain about my collection of scarves (and I have literally hundreds in every color and fabric imaginable) is my cat Luna, and she doesn't really seem to mind much. I just have to be careful to avoid riding in convertibles, lest I meet a fate similar to Duncan's. (Her scarf caught on the car's rear axle, breaking her neck. Who knew style could be so dangerous?)

WORKSHEET:

Work Survey

Are there any clothing restrictions or dress codes you must follow at work?

How would you describe your work environment?

What do your co-workers wear?

What does your boss wear?
(Or if you're the boss, what do your employees wear?)

What do you currently wear to work?

What are some things you'd most like to change about your work wardrobe?

Put this worksheet in your style binder, and keep your answers in the back of your mind as you complete the next activity.

ACTIVITY NINE:

Define Your Work Wardrobe

Next is a list of basic work wardrobe items that are traditionally considered "must haves." However, for this activity we'll be replacing the notion of a "must have" list with a "fits my style" list. To the right of each item, jot down some ways to adapt this item to fit within your personal style, or just replace it entirely with something that suits your needs better. Make sure each item is part of the image you wish to convey during the work week. You may wish to describe an item that you pulled from a magazine or catalog during our earlier magazine crawl activity. Feel free to place actual images on this page as well.

You may or may not already have these clothes in your wardrobe. We'll get to that later. For now, just worry about defining it in a way that speaks to your personal style.

Example: White Blouse — a tuxedo shirt, crisp cotton wrap shirt, or a draped silk V-neck blouse.

BASIC ITEM	YOUR INTERPRETATION
1. Basic black pants	Houndstooth Trousers
2. Basic black skirt	Black Pencil Skirt
3. Basic black jacket	Velvet Blazer
4. White blouse	Chambray Button Down
5. Sheath dress	Ponte Knit Scoopneck Dress
6. Sweater	Thin Knit Vneck in fine cotton
7. Upscale cotton tee	Short Sleeve Sweater
8. Vest	Pullover Argyle Sweater Vest
9. Neutral colored skirt	Pinstripe Pencil Skirt
10. Neutral colored / patterned pants	Houndstooth Pencil Skirt (I hate pants)
11. V-neck cardigan sweater	Crew Neck Cardl (with "Jewel Buttons)

Your Turn!

WORKSHEET:

Define Your Work Wardrobe

BASIC ITEM	YOUR INTERPRETATION
1. Basic black pants	
2. Basic black skirt	
3. Basic black jacket	
4. White blouse	
5. Sheath dress	
6. Sweater	
7. Upscale cotton tee	
8. Vest	
9. Neutral colored skirt	
10. Neutral colored / patterned pants	
11. V-neck cardigan sweater	

ACTIVITY TEN:

Define Your Casual Wardrobe

If you're like most women I know, you exert a superhuman amount of energy Monday through Friday into looking your best for work. But then come Saturday, you grab whatever is clean—be it old jeans and a t-shirt or a track suit—and call it a day. But is that really you? I tossed all of my old sweatpants the day I realized that they made feel more lazy and depressed than comfortable. Just because it's not a work day, that doesn't give you an excuse to muck around in baggy pants with a drawstring waistband, does it? Of course not.

I would urge you to use the weekend as a perfect time to play around with your personal style. Maybe this means pairing items you haven't quite gotten used to together, or even breaking in a new pair of shoes. (It's gotta be done some time, right? Blisters are much easier to handle at home than in those long corridors between the parking garage and your office.) Whatever you do, try to infuse as much of your personality as you can into weekend wear. It is, after all, a reflection of who you truly are.

When shifting your personal style into casual gear, make sure to maintain the key ingredients you defined as important. For me, this means selecting fitted clothing made from quality fabrics but that are still comfortable. One way to keep your wardrobe fresh is to move over old work pieces to the weekend. Items that seem a little tired in the workplace can come alive again as weekend wear.

Next is a list of the basic casual wardrobe items. Like we did earlier with the workplace items, consider this a "my style" list rather than a "must have." Make sure each item fits within your defined personal style, but it can be more toned down or relaxed—whatever fits the image you wish to convey on the weekend.

BASIC ITEM	YOUR INTERPRETATION
1. Jeans	Dark Denim Bootcut
2. Casual button-up shirt	Safari Shirt
3. T-shirt	Tanks, Cami and Tees — Soft Cotton. Black
4. Capri pants	No Capris ever — Ponte Knit Skirt
5. Shorts	Denim Pencil Skirt
6. Sweatshirt/Sweatpants	Leggings and Flyaway Cardi
7. Sneakers	Converse
8. Jacket/Coat	Short Khaki Trench and Teal Pea Coat

Your Turn!

WORKSHEET:

Define Your Casual Wardrobe

BASIC ITEM	YOUR INTERPRETATION
1. Jeans	
2. Casual button-up shirt	
3. T-shirt	
4. Capri pants	
5. Shorts	
6. Sweatshirt/ Sweatpants	
7. Sneakers	
8. Jacket/Coat	

ACTIVITY ELEVEN:

Dress Your "Other Selves"

We've covered the work week and the weekend, but there are moments in all of our lives that don't really fit in either category. For our purposes here, let's call those moments our "other selves." For this next exercise, think of all the activities and responsibilities you have in your life that you may need to consider special clothing for. Are you the PTA chair? Do you hold weekly book club meetings in your living room? Do you volunteer during your city's annual jazz festival? Do you and your significant other have a standing date for dinner and dancing? You're probably going to need special clothing for those situations that conveys an even more specific aspect of your personality and personal style.

List all of these roles out on the left column of the worksheet, and then jot down some notes regarding the image you would like to convey to others for each. You can jot down specific items or outfits, or just general notes about how this style differs from your work/casual styles.

ROLE	DESIRED IMAGE
Comic Collector	Spend time digging though old stacks in comic stores and at conventions—but I am NOT wearing a superhero costume! Uniform should be my Geek Tees with other items from my casual stash.
Movie Group	We attend movies and then go to dinner and discuss. But I don't want to just wear casual stuff, because hubby and I use this as a date night. I need something warm enough for the movies, and also dressy enough for a date.

Your Turn!

WORKSHEET:

Dress Your "Other Selves"

ROLE	DESIRED IMAGE

ACTIVITY TWELVE:

Create Your It List

If you spend any time at all reading fashion magazines, you've no doubt encountered the ubiquitous "it list," those wardrobe pieces that all style experts agree a woman simply must have in her closet. These items are listed for you to substitute with your personalized version. Think of ways to adapt each item to the image you wish to convey. Bonus points for matching them up aesthetically with other items you listed above.

Sure, I could have done it different... put my clown in a closet and dressed up in straight clothing. I could have compromised my essence, and swallowed my soul.

~ Wavy Gravy

Example:

IT ITEMS	YOUR VERSION
1. White collar shirt	Striped Button Down
2. Three-piece matching suit	Skirt Suit
3. Little black dress	Little Blue Ponte Sheath
4. Trench coat	Trench Coat
5. Cashmere sweater	Cotton Cardigan
6. Dark wash jeans	Dark Wash Jeans
7. Leather handbag	Slouchy Leather Handbag
8. Strappy sandal	Wedges
9. Black pumps	Red Pumps
10. Stud earrings	No earrings

WORKSHEET:

Create Your It List

IT ITEMS	YOUR VERSION
1. White collar shirt	
2. Three-piece matching suit	
3. Little black dress	
4. Trench coat	
5. Cashmere sweater	
6. Dark wash jeans	
7. Leather handbag	
8. Strappy sandal	
9. Black pumps	
10. Stud earrings	

ACTIVITY THIRTEEN:

Draw Up Your Wardrobe Blueprint

Now that you've covered all of the various dimensions and occasions of your life and considered what you should be wearing during each of them, it's time to record it all below. This sheet will serve as a blueprint for the next section, in which we'll consider the practical aspects of collecting this perfect wardrobe. (If you're already starting to feel anxious or faint, take a deep breath. I'll be there to walk you through it the whole way.)

My unique personal style description is:

The image I wish to portray with that style is:

At work, others would describe my style as:

On the weekend, others would describe my style as:

Here are my four key pieces for:

Work:

1.

2.

3.

4.

My other selves:

1.

2.

3.

4.

Weekend:

1.

2.

3.

4.

My it list:

1.

2.

3.

4.

When you feel like you're ready for some budget and shopping talk, you can move onto the next section!

ACTIVITY THIRTEEN:

Bianca's Wardrobe Blueprint

Now that you've covered all of the various dimensions and occasions of your life and considered what you should be wearing during each of them, it's time to record it all below. This sheet will serve as a blueprint for the next section, in which we'll consider the practical aspects of collecting this perfect wardrobe. (If you're already starting to feel anxious or faint, take a deep breath. I'll be there to walk you through it the whole way.)

My unique personal style description is:

Urban Tea Party

The image I wish to portray with that style is:

I want to project an image that says I'm confident, intelligent, and stylish but also able to have fun.

At work, others would describe my style as:

Professional and approachable.

On the weekend, others would describe my style as:

Quirky, Stylish and Fun. Evening leans to sexy.

Here are my four key pieces for:

Work:
1. *Pencil Skirt*
2. *Teal Blazer*
3. *High end knits*
4. *Cardigan*

Weekend:
1. *Geek Tee*
2. *Cardigan*
3. *Little Ponté Knit Cobalt Dress*
4. *Bootcut Jeans*

My other selves:

1. *Yoga Pants*
2. *Leggings*
3. *Converse*
4. *Tote Bag*

My it list:

1. *Silver Key Necklace*
2. *Oversized Leather Bag*
3. *Suede Pumps*
4. *Trench Coat (Teal)*

When you feel like you're ready for some budget and shopping talk, you can move onto the next section!

SECTION FOUR:
Get Dressed

Putting style theory into style practice

Congratulations for making it this far! We're almost to the finish line. As you probably already noticed, the preceeding three sections have been primarily theoretical in nature, and you've had plenty of time to mentally construct a solid picture of your overall personal style. Depending on your level of motivation and learning style, some of these activities may have been difficult to complete. If so, then even bigger kudos for soldiering through them. But if you're still not 100% sure of where your style stands, now is the time to revisit some of the earlier activities. Having a solid vision of what you want your wardrobe to look like will save you immeasurable time, money, and stress in the long run.

Hopefully you are excited to finally get the chance to put all this theory into practice, but not everyone who reads this book may feel that way. Whereas some readers may have been impatiently longing for the chance to go shopping throughout the earlier sections, perhaps you flew through those activities and now you find yourself freezing up when it comes to following through with the actual act of building a wardrobe. Don't worry—you're not alone. Many women experience anxiety or frustration when it comes to selecting and buying clothing. This may stem from self-esteem issues regarding your body shape or size (trust me—those dressing room mirrors and lights flatter NO ONE), or maybe you find that your financial willpower flies out the window once you step foot in a store. You may even have a simple case of what I like to call IHSS (I Hate Shopping Syndrome), finding the act tedious, time-consuming, and/or completely aggravating. This section will address all of these issues and give you tips and strategies to work through them to achieve wardrobe nirvana.

First we're going to start with an assessment of what you already own, and then we'll tackle the areas of budgeting, shopping, and then finally wardrobe maintenance. If you feel yourself getting nervous, exhausted, or unmotivated at any point during this process, don't be afraid to take it slower. But I urge you to keep at it. Think of how far you've already come!

ACTIVITY FOURTEEN:

State of the Closet

Every woman handles her closet a little differently. The first thing you need to do is identify where you fall on the scale of Natural Culler to Pack Rat. Do you freely dispose of unwanted clothes on a regular basis, or do you keep everything you've ever worn? I personally fall more towards pack rat, though I'm trying to break myself of the habit. Sometimes I'll have a top for a year or two before I find the perfect pants or shoes to go with it. (But it feels so great to finally make use of something rather than toss it out, doesn't it?) a friend of mine is even worse—she still has clothing from high school, including her senior prom dress. I understand the emotional connection to this stuff, but it's not doing a thirty-year old woman any favors hanging around in her everyday closet.

Whether you are a culler or a pack rat, this activity allows for enough flexibility that you won't have to severely alter your closet habits—at least not enough to send you screaming into the office of your therapist or anything. But I urge you to take this opportunity to begin shifting away from any bad closet habits you may be harboring.

We'll start with a simple closet inventory. I'd recommend keeping trash bags handy while going through your things, even if you aren't someone who regularly disposes of clothing. It may shock you how discerning your style eye has already become, and you may be ready to let go of things you never expected.

First, pull all the items out of your closet. You should try on any items that you do not regularly wear or that you have not worn recently, in order to fairly assess whether or not they're keepers. Once everything is laid out, take a deep breath and prepare to tackle the pile.

RENOVATING your wardrobe is also a great time for a hanger makeover. Make sure you have enough for your entire wardrobe, as well as specialty hangers for skirts, pants, and undergarments. I recommend thin flocked hangers, which save space and ensure that your clothing hangs properly. You can usually find them at Target or HSN, and they come in a variety of colors. And take heed of Joan Crawford's advice: no wire! Not only do you run the risk of rust stains on your clothing, they also pinch and crimp clothing much more than plastic or wood hangers.

Preliminary Sort: During this round, you'll want to discard any clothing that doesn't fit or that is too stained, damaged, or worn out to bother cleaning or repairing. You'll obviously want to toss those latter items, but the clothes that are otherwise in good condition but don't fit may be a tougher call. Some items may be able to be tailored, but only keep them if you are *totally sure* you're willing to actually take them somewhere to be altered. Consider donating other items to your local Goodwill.

You'll benefit your community and potentially help less fortunate women acquire clothing for their own wardrobes. And don't forget to get a tax receipt for the donations. If you have pricier pieces or designer items you no longer want or need, contact a local con-signment store about selling these for you. Then you can put this cash back in your clothing budget for new items! When you are done with this first sort, you should only have items that really fit, and that are in good shape left in your pile.

Secondary Sort:
Now that you narrowed down the pile signifi-cantly, it's time to get down to the hard decisions. Go through each item and sort it into one of four smaller piles:

- This fits my new personal style.

- This almost fits my style, and I can certainly make it work.

- This doesn't fit my style, but I am not ready to get rid of it yet.

- This doesn't fit my style, and I can totally let it go.

Once you've gone through everything and you have your four piles, go ahead and put pile four directly into those donation bags. (I also suggest putting them by the front door or directly in your trunk so you're one step closer to actually disposing of them.) That was the easy part!

Items in pile three may be a bit trickier. These are probably perfect-ly wearable items, even though they no longer work with your per-sonal style. Yet for one reason or another, you're still not ready to part with them. (We pack rats know this feeling well.) That's fine—don't stress out or beat yourself up over this—but just be sure to store these in a separate closet or in storage containers under your bed. Keeping them with your daily wardrobe will most likely lead to frustration and confusion in your closet. And this goes against everything that style clarity stands for!

Once you've taken care of these piles, you may wish to return the rest of your clothes to the closet, especially if you're feeling any amount of anxiety or fatigue. If that's the case, don't worry about organizing them. This step will come eventually. For now, take a step back to admire the work you've already accomplished. Savor the fact that you've probably done more for your wardrobe in this short amount of time than you've done in years. Great job!

When you are ready to move on, continue on to the next activity.

....

One arrives at style only with atrocious effort, and with fanatical and devoted stubbornness.

~ Gustave Flaubert

One forges one's style on the terrible anvil of daily deadlines.

~ Emile Zola

....

ACTIVITY FIFTEEN:

Everything Old is New Again

Now that you've edited your closet down to the items that are more in line with your style, it's time to start organizing and assessing. Go ahead and pull out your Key Pieces, Basics, Work Wardrobe, and Casual Wardrobe activity sheets that we completed in Section Three. Review each item, and your notes on what you planned to do for each. In the first column on the following worksheet, write down your interpretation of each item from those sheets.

For each item, determine if something you already have in your closet fits perfectly in that spot. If so, great! Write down a short description of it on the following worksheet. If you have something that is close—not quite perfect, but it will work for now—go ahead and list that in the second column. You can always keep your eyes open for potential replacements during the shopping phase. If you have nothing in your wardrobe that fits a particular category, check the "needed" box.

Example:

CATEGORY	MY INTERPRE-TATION	ITEM I OWN	THIS WILL DO	NEEDED
Key Pieces	Suede Blazer	Camel Banana Republic Suede Blazer		
Basics	White wrap Blouse		Ann Taylor Wrap	
Basics	Denim Pencil Skirt			x

WORKSHEET:

Wardrobe Inventory

CATEGORY	MY INTERPRE-TATION	ITEM I OWN	THIS WILL DO	NEEDED

Establishing your clothing budget

Taking on a project as major as a style overhaul unfortunately comes with a price tag. But how big that price tag ends up being is entirely up to you. You may have a large number of things on that "need" list from the previous activity, but be sure not to confuse a "need in my closet" with a real life need. Bills, savings, and the daily necessities of life and your family always come before clothing.

I'm sure I don't have to tell you that money matters can be extremely tricky, and I'm definitely no financial expert myself. It seems like every woman I've ever met (and every man, for that matter) has some sort of issue with budgeting or spending, either in their past or their present situation. Whether it's the easy credit society we're currently living in or a lack of practical financial education in our schools that's the cause for so many bad money habits—who knows. But I also know a number of women who have managed to accumulate great wardrobes without breaking their bank accounts. So how have they done it? Let's take a look at a couple of their secrets:

CASE STUDY 1: *Brenda*

Five years ago and two weeks before my 25th birthday, I officially declared bankruptcy. In just four short years of living on my own, I'd somehow managed to accumulate $30,000 in credit card debt. I was a huge clothes horse, and I just had to have every cute pair of shoes or boutique one-of-a-kind dress I saw. But totally trashing my credit for the next ten years was a huge wakeup call, and I made a promise to myself that I would never let it happen again. I took a couple of money management courses, and I learned that it was actually possible to stick to a budget *and* remain highly fashionable. Now I save $100 a month and go on a shopping spree (cash only) every three or four months. Maybe I'll just have enough to buy a new jacket or suede boots, but those items are a million times more significant to me now that I know they are 100% earned and paid for. I've also found that it's almost *harder* to find items worthy of purchase when I have a set amount of cash to spend. I'd be lying if I said it all didn't take a major period of adjustment, but I'm definitely happier now than when I was living on borrowed fashion!

CASE STUDY 2: *Rebecca*

I get constant compliments on my wardrobe, and every time someone says, "Great shoes!" or "Where did you get that blazer?" I have to smile. I usually just say, "Oh gosh, this old thing? I barely remember!" But nine times out of ten, I've found it at the Goodwill or some other secondhand store. The fact that I don't openly share this with other women doesn't come from shame or embarrassment; rather it's all about defense! I work hard searching for these great finds, and I'm not about to give away my secret to potential competition! My favorite hunting grounds are nearby upscale suburbs. You'd be amazed by the nearly new designer pieces I've found there. Just last weekend I nabbed a pair of Coach shoes with not a scratch on the soles. And sure, it may take a little extra time and patience when compared to regular shopping, but I consider it a worthy pastime. And I have a killer wardrobe that cost a mere fraction of what its original owners paid to show for my treasure hunting skills!

CASE STUDY 3: *Rose*

I'm a coffee shop barista and college student, so I'm not exactly rolling around in a bed full of hundred dollar bills every night. Luckily, my style is extremely casual. I prefer shopping at places like Old Navy and Target for 90% of my clothes, not only because it's cheap, but also because I honestly love the styles.

Hey—not every girl has to be Sienna Miller, right? So maybe the seams of my t-shirts come undone within months, or the pockets of my jeans rip out with startling consistency, but by that time I'm probably sick of those clothes anyway. I just look at it as a perfect excuse to go shopping again! I'm sure I'll upgrade my style after I graduate and start a professional career in journalism, but for now I am perfectly happy with my wardrobe.

It goes without saying that every woman's financial situation is different, but there are a few questions that everyone needs to honestly consider when deciding on a practical and sustainable clothing budget:

1. After you've paid all of your major expenses, how much extra can you comfortably set aside from each paycheck to put into your clothing fund? This doesn't have to be major. Even $20 per paycheck adds up over time, depending on how often you shop and what kinds of clothing you're looking for.

2. What is most important to you when purchasing clothing: cost or quality? That Target top may be cute and cheap, but it's probably not going to last more than three or four wearings before it pills, stretches out, or unravels in the wash. Personally, I prefer to spend more money on quality items, especially mainstays like shoes and blazers. But this also means you may not be able to purchase all of your items at once.

3. Are there areas of your life where you can tighten your belt to help free up extra clothing funds? Perhaps you can live with a regular $2 cup of coffee instead of your $4 mocha? Brown bag your lunch instead of eating out every day? My finances significantly improved when I had the epiphany that I could spend the same

amount on an entire bag of bagels and tub of cream cheese that I used to spend on a single bagel and spread from the café down the street.

Whatever your situation, don't be overwhelmed if you can't get every item your new style requires right away. It may be frustrating now that you can see the finish line, but remember: you're in the process of developing your ultimate style, not completing a 24-hour makeover show!

ACTIVITY SIXTEEN:

Shopping Prep

Now that you have an idea of what pieces you need to purchase and a clear idea of your budget, you still need to do a little more preparatory work before you head out into the field for your hunt.

Highlight the "needed" items from the previous worksheet and consider how much you're willing to spend on each one. You may want to do a little Internet intel to get a better idea of what these items cost if you aren't sure.

Primary shopping list

WHAT DO I NEED?	HOW MUCH CAN I SPEND?

Again, depending on your clothing budget, the actual purchasing of these items may take place all at once or over the course of the next few months (or longer). Some items may be out of season and will have to wait. No pressure. As we discussed earlier, only you can accurately gauge how much you're able to invest in your wardrobe at any given time. But now at least you have a prioritized list of items to stick to.

After you have developed your primary shopping list and filled in your must haves, start a secondary shopping list. Use the "this will do" items that you eventually want to replace with new pieces. Keep this list handy any time you have a little extra clothing cash around, or feel free to tackle it once you complete your primary shopping list.

Secondary shopping list

WHAT DO I WANT TO REPLACE?	HOW SOON DO I NEED IT?	HOW MUCH SHOULD I SPEND?

Ready, set, shop!

Finally, it's time to go shopping. You're either totally psyched, full of dread and/or denial, or somewhere in between. Personally, I used to love shopping when I was a teenager, and I spent an obscene amount of my free time during junior high and high school wandering aimlessly through stores or hanging out at the mall food court with my friends. But somewhere between the ages of 18 and 22, I developed a dislike of shopping. I'm not sure why, but it seemed more like a chore than a pleasure. It was in my late twenties when I put this whole program to practice that I finally found a love for shopping again. Here are a few tips to help discover some of that "treasure hunt" feeling that might be inside you:

TIP #1: START SMALL AND HAVE ONE OR TWO TARGET ITEMS IN MIND.

It can be extremely daunting to enter a gigantic department store (or even a small boutique) with a generalized "I need to buy clothing" mission. The key is to identify just a few things you're on the lookout for (i.e. the perfect pair of black pants and a neutral pencil skirt) and stick ONLY to those items. Ignore everything else. This will help ward off fatigue and keep you from overspending.

TIP #2: TAKE FREQUENT BREAKS.

You may want to get your shopping over as soon as possible, especially if you have IHSS, but you have to remember to pace yourself. Schedule plenty of time to shop, and treat it as it truly is: leisure time. Treat yourself to a manicure or a pedicure in between stores, if that's your style. Or just sit on a bench and people watch. It's free, and you may even pick up a few fashion pointers from other shoppers!

TIP #3: EAT A MEAL BEFORE YOU HEAD OUT FOR A WHOLE DAY OF SHOPPING.

I'm not really a breakfast person. Usually I head out the door in the morning with a belly full of coffee and *maybe* a single-serving of yogurt if I'm feeling particularly ambitious. This makes me highly susceptible to blood sugar crashes. And anyone who has known me longer than a few months can tell you—when this happens, I am completely useless in every way (not to mention extremely, irrationally irritable). There's nothing worse than standing at a rack of clothing and feeling that wave of nausea or light-headedness wash over you. Well—maybe knowing your only immediate food option is MSG-laden Chinese food or a greasy slice of pizza. Do yourself (and those poor defenseless store clerks) a favor and ensure you have the fuel to accomplish your shopping mission!

TIP #4: STAY HYDRATED.

This is an extension of Tip #2. Keep a water bottle in your purse or bag (or an energy or sports drink if you're so inclined—I don't judge) at all times. The recycled air in most stores can really sap your fluids.

TIP #5: DO YOUR HAIR AND MAKEUP.

It may be tempting just to roll out of bed on a Saturday morning, pull your hair back in a ponytail, and head out for a shopping trip, but it's crucial that you resist this urge. You don't have to pull out the full formal look, but I do suggest styling your hair and doing your makeup as you normally would for work. We've all experienced the hundred-fold magnifying power of florescent lights and full-length multi-angle mirrors, right? Once you get into the dressing room, you want as few distractions from the clothing as possible.

TIP #6: BRING A FRIEND.

Not only does having a shopping buddy allow you to recapture some of that pre-teen mall magic, but you'll also have a second set of eyes to keep you away from questionable items and impulse buys. But make sure this person is fully prepared and up for the task, including proper feeding and hydration. (Bonus points if you can trust him or her enough to tell you the honest truth about how your butt looks in those jeans.)

Now let's say you've located whatever item you've been searching for—that pair of black pants that's a "must have," for instance. Here are the questions you need to ask yourself in the dressing room before you lay down the cash for it:

1. Does it fit perfectly?

2. Do you love the color?

3. Does it fit your established style?

4. Does it support your image definition?

5. Will it work with other items you already own?

6. Is it versatile enough to adapt to at least three different outfits?

Remember, you're rebuilding your wardrobe and your style from the ground up here. It's very important that you stick to the standards and guidelines you've established thus far in this workbook. The time for settling is over. You owe it to yourself to make sure you love everything you bring home.

A note on sales...

Everyone loves a sale, right? Especially in this economy, you can sometimes find some extraordinary deals at some stores. But we have to make sure to keep it all in perspective. Sale items are meant to be hidden treasure that other shoppers missed out on, and not just cheap closet filler!

Believe me, I have had my share of flops when it comes to the sales rack, and have a sale-specific checklist I always run through in addition to the questions above.

1. Is this piece truly necessary, or am I just swayed by the price tag?

I try and think of at least 3 outfits using the item and items **already in my closet.** If I can't do it quickly, it goes back on the rack. If it is a crossover piece (both work and casual), then it's an immediate keeper.

2. Is this item already somewhere in my closet?

I am notorious for picking up black cardigans. I already have a short sleeve cardi, a 3/4 length one and a long sleeve one. Even though I consciously know they're my weakness, I am still inexplicably drawn to them! But once I ask myself this question, it gets much harder to justify exactly why THIS black cardigan will fill a need one of the other three doesn't already fill.

3. Is this truly a quality item or just junk?

Is there some flaw in the fabric or the construction that kept it from being sold at full price? Just because it's a sale item, that's not an excuse to purchase something that doesn't look or fit exactly right. If it's a top, are the sleeves binding? If it's a skirt or a pair of pants, can I sit down and bend over in it comfortably? If I put it on and it looks and feels like heaven? Keeper. If anything is itchy, uncomfortable, or not 100% like new—back on the rack it goes, no matter the markdown.

One important bit of advice: whether your purchases are on sale or not, ALWAYS familiarize yourself with the store's return policy. Even though you gave careful consideration to the purchase of each item in the store, that doesn't guarantee you'll like it or want to keep it once you get it home. More often than not, there will be special policies regarding sale items, so be sure to keep a lookout for the fine print. And beware of anything marked FINAL or CLEAR-ANCE. These items usually cannot be returned or exchanged under any circumstances.

Still not ready to dive into the shopping experience? Maybe a little advice from some women who have tackled their own shopping demons will push you along.

CASE STUDY 1: *Greta*

For most of my adult life, I've suffered from extreme dressing room anxiety, mostly because of body issues. I find it extra frustrating because on a typical day-to-day basis, my self-esteem is pretty darn solid. It's not like I'm a supermodel or anything, but I'm generally happy with my shape and size. But get me in the dressing room, and it's like some long-hidden body dysmorphic disorder emerges in my psyche. It's all I can manage to tell myself that I really don't look that horrible, and just purchase the clothes and get the heck out of there. Ultimately, I've found that the only way I can maintain my wardrobe and my sanity is to shop online through stores that post extremely detailed size and measurement info and offer free return shipping. It may limit my choices a little bit, but I've made it work.

CASE STUDY 2: *Val*

I really don't mind the act of shopping, but for the longest time I found it very difficult to find anything I really like. I have no explanation for this, as my style isn't totally out of the mainstream

FOR POSTERITY'S SAKE

Thanks to smart phone technology, it's now easier than ever to keep tabs on your closet inventory. There are dozens of apps available that allow you to photograph and organize individual clothing items, and it's a great resource to have when you're out shopping for new pieces. A few possibilities include Outfit Diary, Touch Closet, My Fashion Closet, and Stylish Girl. Most of these are free or just 99¢, but some apps with more features can cost as much as ten dollars. Keeping such detailed records of your clothing could also benefit you in the unfortunate case of a home fire or burglary.

or anything. I just get so... uninspired when I shop. A few years ago, I was lucky enough to come across one particular store that seems pretty in sync with my personal style. Their clothes may not be a perfect match to my tastes every single season, but I can usually find at least four or five strong pieces every time I go. Even better, I know exactly what cut and size I am there, so I can purchase through their online store anytime I want.

CASE STUDY 3: *Michelle*

My shopping problem is that I like it WAY too much. I am a classic impulse buyer, especially where sales are concerned. My last disaster involved an Ann Taylor Loft Outlet Store and four variations of plaid, mid-thigh schoolgirl skirts. I didn't even get all the way home before I had my patented "Really, Michelle?" moment. And of course they were non-returnable! Since then I've stuck hard and fast to Tip #1 above. I don't leave the house without a list of one or two very specific items, and I will not stray from it—no matter what temptations hang on that clearance rack.

Maintaining your new wardrobe

Now that you've started to purchase those all-important items to round out your perfect wardrobe, it may be tempting to stick them in the closet and call it a day—but not so fast. If you want your wardrobe to stay cohesive and versatile, you need to integrate the new items right away. As soon as you bring them home, take a quick inventory of your closet and try to create at least three outfits using the new piece as the focus. You might want to take some photos or jot down some notes to remember these combinations. Keep all of this in your style binder for future reference.

Once you've organized every item inside your closet to your satisfaction, it's important to keep some tools at hand to keep your wardrobe in top shape. Consider the following:

1. A small sewing kit.

You don't have to be an expert seamstress to sew on a button or fix a hem. If you're nervous around a needle and thread, there are plenty of YouTube videos that can show you how it's done. Consider keeping a dependable tailor and shoe repair service in your contacts for the bigger emergencies.

2. A box for all those extra buttons.

Mine sits right on top of my dresser for easy access. It's an extra smart time saver to label each baggie/envelope with the garment the button goes with. And when those buttons fall off or even get loose, REPAIR THEM! It's no use going to all this trouble developing a style just to end up looking like a slob!

3. A full length mirror.

Bathroom mirrors are great, but your outfit doesn't stop at your waist. Check yourself out daily, and turn around as well. And remember: shoes can make or break the outfit, so don't wait until you're heading out the door to throw them on.

4. A Steamer.

I bought a $40 steamer from Amazon.com and I love that bad boy. Within just a few minutes, unsightly wrinkles completely disappear. And if you were out at a smoky nightclub last night in that velvet blazer you now need to wear to work, the steamer can eliminate most of the smell.

Final thoughts

By now, you should be well on your way to having not only a well-defined sense of personal style, but also a cohesive and well-maintained closet that reflects it. On the next few pages you'll find a Full Wardrobe Template. Keep this worksheet handy as your wardrobe evolves or becomes even more refined in the future. Just like some cooks like to keep a fully stocked kitchen, over time you will want to have a fully stocked wardrobe.

Over the course of developing and writing this workbook, I've had the pleasure to meet many women who came along on my journey and discovered their own style clarity. You've met some of the most memorable through the case studies and other anecdotes I've shared in these pages. I've gotten such positive feedback from so many people, including some who have used this opportunity for even deeper self-examination and change.

....

Finding style clarity gave me the willpower and confidence
to lose 45 pounds. I had to buy a totally new wardrobe
a second time, but hey—totally worth it!

~ Candl H.

Focusing on my personal style was just the thing I needed
to get over a bitter and messy divorce. Now I'm just hoping
to run into him so he can see what he gave up!

~ Susan B.

I didn't just stop at style clarity. I went all the way for a total
makeover, including a dramatic haircut and color change.
My co-workers are still in shock, and I love it!

~ Diane P.

....

I would love to hear about your journey towards style clarity.

Please email me at: bianca@styleclarity.com
and let me know how it went!

The Complete Wardrobe Checklist

Skirt Wardrobe

☐ All Season Work Skirt

☐ All Season Work Skirt

☐ Day to Night Skirt

☐ Denim Skirt

☐ Weekend Skirt

☐ Weekend Skirt

Pants Wardrobe

☐ Summer Work Pants

☐ Summer Work Pants

☐ Winter Work Pants

☐ All Season Weekend

☐ All Season Weekend

☐ Evening Pants

T-Shirt Wardrobe

☐ L/S White Tee

☐ S/S White Tee

☐ L/S Black Tee

☐ S/S Black Tee

☐ Striped Tee

☐ Polo

Tops Wardrobe

☐ Work Shirt

☐ Work Shirt

☐ Work Shirt

☐ Work Shirt

☐ Day to Night Shirt

☐ Weekend Shirt

☐ Weekend Shirt

☐ Weekend Shirt

☐ Evening Shirt

Sweater Wardrobe

☐ Fitted Pullover

☐ Fitted Pullover

☐ Cardigan

☐ Cardigan

☐ Weekend Sweater

☐ Evening Sweater

Casual Pants

☐ Pair of jeans that fits with heels

☐ Pair of jeans that fits with flats

☐ White Jeans

☐ Corduroys

☐ Fun Pair of Jeans

☐ A Pair to Wreck

Jacket Wardrobe

☐ Good Wool Blazer

☐ Short Jacket

☐ Jean Jacket

☐ Velvet Blazer

☐ Summer Jacket

☐ Corduroy Jacket

☐ Winter Coat

Dress Wardrobe

☐ Work Dress

☐ Work Dress

☐ Weekend Dress

☐ Weekend Dress

☐ Daytime Party

☐ Evening Dress

Suit Wardrobe

☐ Classic Suit

☐ Classic Suit

☐ Skirt Suit

☐ Evening Suit

Shoe Wardrobe

☐ Work Heels

☐ Work Flats

☐ Casual Shoes

☐ Strappy Sandals

☐ Flat Sandals

☐ Evening Shoe

☐ Boots

Handbags Wardrobe

☐ Everyday Bag

☐ Work Bag

☐ Casual Tote

☐ Evening Bag

Acknowledgements

My amazing and stylish daughter, Ariana and my patient and supportive husband, Nabil. They have been my rock and the best fans a girl could ask for. My mom and my sister again—The entire extended Chesimard family, all very stylish people. Love you all and thank you!

My editor, Erin Foster Hartley—she kept me sane and balanced during the process, between numerous rewrites, my brilliant 4am ideas and a myriad of interesting grammar choices, she helped this book take shape—I couldn't have done it without her! Also, Melanie Brown, PhD—what an eagle eye for a missing hyphen! Thank you so much!

This next group of people supported me very early on in the project, and I would be remiss if I didn't mention each one:

Brett Bjornsen — G+ plusvegas.com

Christina Gill

Concetta Bommarito

Christopher BAMF Lira

Donyé Robinson, I.

Elisabeth Gilliam

Emily Ecycle Wells

Jenny Gibbons

K. V. Gaines

Kisha Machen—SIO Fitness

Lia M Lorelli

Monique

Samuel F. Reynolds

Sean C. Thomas

Selena Strain

Shareef Jackson

Shari Weinman Crespy

Shawn Marie Story-Lowe

Stephanie M. Stroup

Tim

Tonya Lockamy

William D Lipira

Thank you to everyone who helped out with this book.

Made in the USA
San Bernardino, CA
13 March 2016